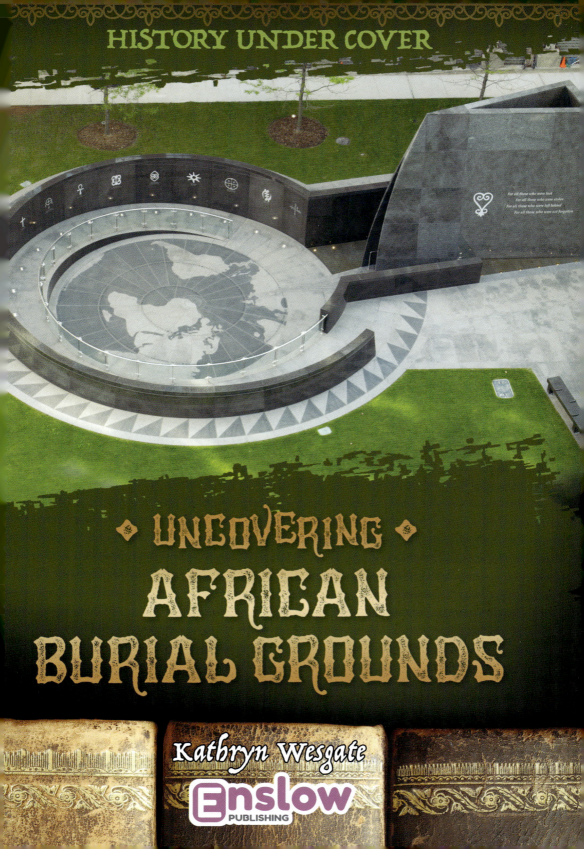

Please visit our website, www.enslow.com. For a free color catalog of all our high-quality books, call toll free 1-800-398-2504 or fax 1-877-980-4454.

Cataloging-in-Publication Data
Names: Wesgate, Kathryn.
Title: Uncovering African burial grounds / Kathryn Wesgate.
Description: New York : Enslow Publishing, 2023. | Series: History under cover | Includes glossary and index.
Identifiers: ISBN 9781978528741 (pbk.) | ISBN 9781978528765 (library bound) | ISBN 9781978528758 (6pack) | ISBN 9781978528772 (ebook)
Subjects: LCSH: African Burial Ground (New York, N.Y.)–Juvenile literature.
Classification: LCC F128.9.N4 2023 | DDC 363.7'509747–dc23

Published in 2023 by
Enslow Publishing
29 East 21st Street
New York, NY 10010

Copyright © 2023 Enslow Publishing

Portions of this work were originally authored by Therese M. Shea and published as *The African Burial Ground*. All new material this edition authored by Kathryn Wesgate.

Designer: Leslie Taylor
Editor: Kate Mikoley

Photo credits: Cover, p. 29 Carol M. Highsmith/LOC.com.; series art (scrolls) Magenta10/Shutterstock.com, series art (back cover leather texture) levan828/Shutterstock.com; series art (front cover books) RMMPPhotography/Shutterstock.com; series art (title font) MagicPics/Shutterstock.com; series art (ripped inside pgs) kaczor58/Shutterstock.com; p. 4 Commons.wikimedia.org; p. 5 Mario Suriani/APimages.com; p. 7 Sendo Serra/Shutterstock.com; p. 8 Commons.wikimedia.org; pp. 9, 10, 22, 24 Bebeto Matthews/APimages.com; p. 11 (top) Eric Glenn/Shutterstock.com; p. 11 (middle) Elnur/Shutterstock.com; p. 12 Lebrecht Music & Arts/Alamy.com; p. 13 The Eno collection of New York City views/Digital Public Library of America-dp.la; p. 14 IanDagnall Computing/Alamy.com; p. 15 Ilya Rab/Shutterstock.com; p. 15 (inset) Morphart Creation/Shutterstock.com; p. 16 The Picture Art Collection/Alamy.com; p. 17 North Wind Picture Archives/Alamy.com; p. 18 FLHC 5/Alamy.com; p. 19 1776 map/Commons.wikimedia.org; p. 20 Balfore Archive Images/Alamy.com; p. 21 (inside Museum) Commons.wikimedia.org; p. 21 (inset, aerial view) Commons.wikimedia.org; p. 23 Miljan Mladenovic/Shutterstock.com; p. 25 Mike Derer/APimages.com; p. 26 (monument) Commons.wikimedia.org; p. 27 (monument detail) Commons.wikimedia.org; pp. 28/29 (timeline art) K3Star/Shutterstock.com.

All rights reserved. No part of this book may be reproduced in any form without permission in writing from the publisher, except by a reviewer.

Printed in the United States of America

Some of the images in this book illustrate individuals who are models. The depictions do not imply actual situations or events.

CPSIA compliance information: Batch #CSENS23: For further information, contact Enslow Publishing, New York, New York, at 1-800-398-2504.

Find us on

Uncovering History 4

Studying the Remains 6

The People Behind the Bones 8

Slavery in New York 12

The Burial Ground's Land 18

What to Do with the Remains? 22

A Final Memorial 24

A Place to Remember 26

Glossary 30

For More Information 31

Index 32

Words in the glossary appear in bold or highlighted type the first time they are used in the text.

Uncovering History

In 1991, one of the most important archaeological discoveries of the 20th century was made in New York City. While preparing for the construction of a new federal office building in a hectic part of the city, a skeleton was found. Further **excavation** exposed another skeleton, and another, and then another. Altogether, the bones of more than 400 men, women, and children were exhumed, or unearthed. Investigations revealed the bones belonged to

Africans who lived during the 17th and 18th centuries. This area of New York had been a burial ground set aside for both free and enslaved Africans during colonial times.

Today, this location is known as the African Burial Ground. It shows us a lot about what life was like in colonial New York for both free and enslaved Africans.

African Burial Ground excavation site, New York City

~ Preparing to Build ~

Before a building is constructed, an environmental impact study is often done. Professionals study how the building might affect the people, animals, and plant life surrounding it. Another part of the study looks into the history of the site. Historical maps indicated that the plot on which the federal building was to be built had been a burial ground. However, it was thought that previous construction projects would have "obliterated any remains." Crews learned this was untrue when they uncovered the first body below the corner of Broadway and Reade Street in Lower Manhattan.

Studying the Remains

People knew that much could be learned from studying the remains. Once removed, the bones were brought to a nearby college. Then, the Cobb Laboratory in Washington, DC, was chosen to study them. This respected research institution is connected to Howard University, a historically Black school.

Human remains can reveal much about what a person's life was like, including how they ate. For example, scientists examined the teeth of the people found in the African Burial Ground. Faults in the teeth were evidence of a poor diet. Comparing these teeth to the teeth of Africans who remained in Africa their whole life revealed that the people found in the burial ground were more likely to have suffered from **malnutrition**. This was likely a result of poor diets and unhealthy living conditions.

~ Lots of Lead ~

Many of the bones studied from the burial ground had something in common: very high levels of lead. Experts found that the longer the person had lived in New York, the higher the lead levels in their bones tended to be. Lead poisoning can result in low energy, small appetite, headaches, slow body growth, hearing loss, and other health problems. It's especially harmful to children. While there's no way of knowing for sure where the lead came from, likely possibilities include certain drinks and containers used to store food.

Each human skeleton found at the site tells a story about that person's life and the world they lived in.

The People Behind the Bones

This sculpture is based on scientific recreations of what three of the people whose skeletons were exhumed may have looked like.

Studying human remains can help us get to know the people they belonged to. Learning about the bones in the African Burial Ground helped us find and tell some of their stories.

Scientists recorded each exhumed skeleton's identifying features and condition. Each skeleton was given a number. For example, "Burial 254" was the remains of a child believed to be between 3 and 6 years old. A piece of silver jewelry thought to be an earring or a piece of a necklace was found with the child.

"Burial 205" was the skeleton of a young woman with more fractures, or broken bones, than any of the other skeletons examined. She had shattered bones in her arms, legs, backbone, skull, and other places. Scientists don't know if these were from a terrible accident or a violent attack.

Photographs of some of the unearthed remains can be viewed at the African Burial Ground National Monument Visitor Center in New York City.

~ Learn Their Stories ~

"Burial 25" was a woman in her early 20s. A musket ball in her rib cage revealed that her death was violent. Scientists believe the ball was fired at her back. She was either running away, or her attacker surprised her. Broken bones in her face indicate that she was struck. New bone growth suggests she lived several more days before dying.

Another person, "Burial 259," might have been a woman dressed in men's clothing. She may have been disguising herself to get hired for certain kinds of work or to escape her enslaver.

9

Anthropologists and other scientists from the African Burial Ground Project made many shocking discoveries. One of the biggest was that half of the Africans whose remains were found and studied didn't even live to become teenagers. Others lived only a short time in the colony before they died. Undoubtedly, their hard lives had much to do with this. Their skeletons reflected a life of hardship: injured and broken bones tell of being overworked—or even worked to death.

Many people don't think of New York as having had many enslaved people. However, enslaved Africans were in fact forced to do many kinds of labor in the busy seaport. The discovery of the burial ground brought new attention to the role of enslaved Africans in the growth and building of colonial New York.

Today, people still remember those buried at the African Burial Ground in New York City.

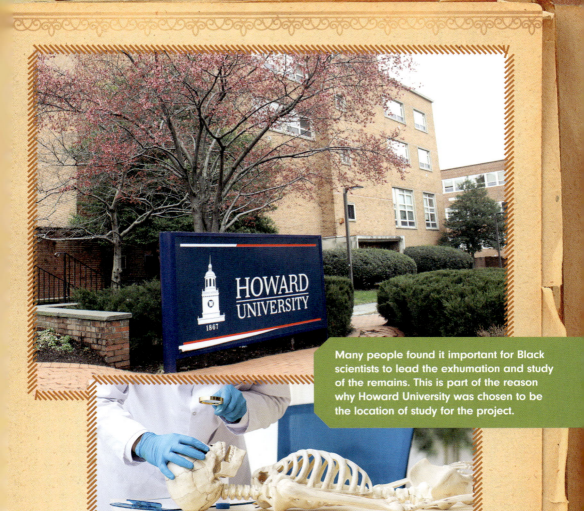

Many people found it important for Black scientists to lead the exhumation and study of the remains. This is part of the reason why Howard University was chosen to be the location of study for the project.

~ All Sorts of Scientists ~

Many kinds of scientists were involved in unearthing and examining the skeletal remains found at New York City's African Burial Ground. Anthropologists are scientists who study humans, their origins, and their ways of life, both past and present. Archaeologists focus on studying past human life by examining bones, tools, and other objects. Other types of scientists involved in the African Burial Ground Project included geneticists and chemists.

Slavery in New York

History books sometimes make it seem as though slavery was only a problem in the American South. However, people were enslaved in the North too. In fact, enslaved Africans were a major presence in New York.

The Dutch first established a trading post that they called New Amsterdam in 1626 on the tip of the island that's now Manhattan. It became part of the Dutch colony of New Netherland. The Dutch West India Company brought enslaved people from the Caribbean for building projects and to work in the fur trade. In 1655, the first enslaved people directly from Africa were brought to New Amsterdam.

This image shows the first auction of enslaved people in New Amsterdam in 1655.

This image shows the view of New Amsterdam from the south in 1671. *Novum Amsterodamum* is Latin for New Amsterdam.

Much labor was involved in building a colony. Land was cleared for houses, and docks were needed for ships. Enslaved people were forced to do much of this work.

~ Few Rights ~

Enslaved people may have made up as much as 40 percent of the population of New Netherland. While enslaved people in general had very few rights, those under Dutch rule in the colony had some that enslaved people in other places didn't. Their lives were still extremely difficult, but they could marry, work for themselves when not working for their owners, and own some property. They could also sue whites. There are records of an enslaved man named Anthony Portuguese suing a white businessman in 1638 after the businessman's dog hurt Anthony's pig. Perhaps even more surprising was the fact that Anthony won.

In 1644, some enslaved people in the area were given what was referred to as "half-freedom" and were allowed to farm north of New Amsterdam. They had **petitioned** for their freedom because they had performed forced labor for years and said they had been promised freedom. While they did receive some freedom, it came with conditions. In return for their "half-freedom," they agreed to share some of their grain and livestock. They also promised to work at times for the West India Company.

New Netherland was conquered by England in 1664 and shortly after became the British colony of New York. New Amsterdam, now New York City, grew into a busy commercial center. By 1700, the city had almost 5,000 residents. By 1730, at least 15 percent of the residents were enslaved Africans.

New York was named for James II, the duke of York and later king of England. He is shown here.

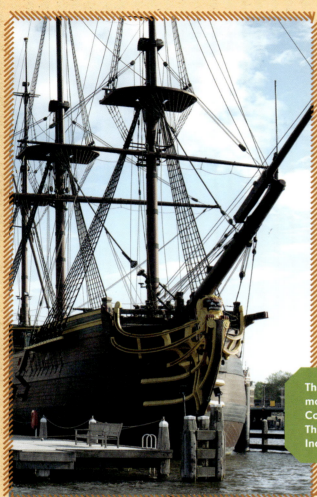

Dutch West India Company flag

The Dutch West India Company was modeled after the Dutch East India Company, its more-successful counterpart. This ship is a recreation of the Dutch East India Company's ship, the *Amsterdam*.

~ The Dutch West India Company ~

New Netherland was the second colony to bring enslaved people to what is now the United States. The first was Virginia. However, unlike Virginia and other colonies, those first enslaved in New Netherland were not enslaved by individuals or families. They were enslaved by a business partly funded by the Dutch government. The Dutch West India Company, also known simply as the West India Company, was a Dutch trading company formed in 1621. In its day, it had even more power than companies such as Microsoft and General Motors have today.

15

Enslaved people were viewed by their enslavers as property to be bought and sold. This is a bill from such a sale made in 1785.

With English rule, the treatment of enslaved people was harsher. They had fewer rights than under the Dutch. For example, no more than three Africans were allowed to meet in public. Enslaved Africans also had **curfews**. They weren't allowed to attend funerals after dark, which was a big part of funeral practices from West Africa. These laws were a response to fears of **rebellions**. The British also made it harder for enslaved people to be freed.

In the early 1700s, a slave market opened in Manhattan. Enslaved people were brought on ships from Africa, some younger than 13 years old. By the end of the 18th century, nearly 80 percent of Black people in New York City and nearby Westchester County were enslaved.

This image shows a slave market on the waterfront of New York City.

~ Rebellions—or Not? ~

Slave rebellions were ways in which enslaved people fought for their freedom. They included actions such as raiding and attacking. During an uprising in New York City in 1712, 23 enslaved people set fire to a building, attacked several white people, and ran away. They were later captured and killed.

In 1741, fires in New York City were blamed on enslaved Black people. Their accuser, an **indentured servant**, was promised her freedom for naming the wrongdoers. Several enslaved people were burned at the stake. Many historians believe the accuser was lying.

The Burial Ground's Land

In early New York City, neither enslaved Africans nor free Blacks were allowed to be buried in cemeteries with white people. In fact, they couldn't even be buried within the city. In 1673, a Dutch woman named Sara Van Borsum permitted some land she owned outside the city to become a burial ground for Africans.

We can tell that enslaved people had funeral services similar to colonists of the time from how they were buried. They were placed in wooden **coffins** with arms folded or placed at their sides. Sometimes, items such as coins and beads were placed in coffins too. The coffin was positioned in the ground so the head was facing west, a Christian tradition. As the burial ground became crowded, coffins were buried on top of coffins.

This image shows what the African Burial Ground may have looked like when it was in use.

This map shows a plan of New York City from 1776. The burial ground was located near the area labeled "Fresh Water."

~ Sara Van Borsum ~

While historians don't know everything about Sara Van Borsum, they do know some facts. Her stepfather, a minister, was known for supporting the education of Black children and for opposing wars with Native Americans.

Sara herself was a translator who received the burial ground land for helping the government communicate with Native Americans. She also received a large amount of land in New Jersey from Native Americans. One might assume by her actions that Sara was against slavery. However, that is not true. She herself enslaved at least six people.

The African Burial Ground closed in 1794. The next year, the African Society, a group established by free African Americans, opened a new cemetery for Black people in the city.

By the time the African Burial Ground closed, the city had greatly expanded. Pressure was put on "unused" sites such as cemeteries to be used for construction. In 1795, the African Burial Ground was divided up and sold. Since it was located in a ravine, it took about 25 feet (7.6 m) of fill to level it. Over the years, buildings were built, torn down, and built again. When excavation began in 1991 for the new federal building, the site of the African Burial Ground was just a parking lot. No one expected the remains to still be found at the site.

While it was known the area had once been a burial ground, experts thought the years of building would have destroyed any remains. Workers were surprised when they started finding skeletons.

Today, people can learn more about the African Burial Ground at its visitor center, shown above. It's located near the African Burial Ground National Monument, left.

~ The First Non-Native New Yorker ~

The first non-native person to live in what is now Manhattan was a man named Jan (or Juan) Rodrigues. He was a free Black sailor from Santo Domingo in the Dominican Republic. His mother was African and his father was Portuguese. He arrived with a trading voyage in 1613. Soon, he learned the language of the Lenape people who lived there. When the others he arrived with got back on the ship to the Netherlands, Rodrigues stayed behind. He opened a trading post and later helped the Dutch trade with the Native Americans.

What to Do with the Remains?

Many people didn't want the remains that were rediscovered to be removed. They felt that exhuming the bodies and rebuilding over the site disrespected the memories of the people buried there. When Howard University took control of the excavation and research, officials promised the public that the site would be handled with reverence.

So what happened with the plans for the 34-story federal building that began the excavation in the first place? It was decided that the tower of the building would be built, but not the pavilion over the graves. Further, any new building in the burial ground area would require special permission. Still, many felt more needed to be done to recognize this special place. In 1993, the African Burial Ground was declared a National Historic Landmark.

Today, Bryant Park is one New York City's most well-known parks. In the 1800s, it was a burial ground for the city's poor residents.

~ History Below Your Feet ~

It may seem unusual that a cemetery could be hidden for hundreds of years. However, the African Burial Ground isn't the only final resting place to be covered, paved, and forgotten about while New York City expanded. According to the Parks Department, more than 50 of the city's parks are on lands that were once used for burials. Union Square, Washington Square Park, and Bryant Park are just a few examples. In other places where construction took place, remains were either moved or left where they were, forever buried under buildings and streets.

A Final Memorial

For more than a decade, the bones that had been removed from the African Burial Ground were studied. Finally, in 2003, each of the 419 human skeletal remains were prepared for reburial. Each skeleton was placed into a hand-carved wooden coffin made in the African country of Ghana.

In September 2003, the remains began their journey from Washington, DC, back to New York. Four people were chosen to symbolize those buried in the African Burial Ground: an adult male, an adult female, a male child, and a female child. They stopped in cities along the way where enslaved Africans had worked. The remains were set into their final resting place at the African Burial Ground Memorial Site on October 4, 2003. In 2006, the African Burial Ground was named a U.S. National Monument, making it protected by the government.

Throughout the journey from Washington, DC, to New York, many people gathered to pay their respects to those being laid to rest.

~ Marking and Honoring the Graves ~

Because of African traditions in other places, anthropologists believe the original graves of the African Burial Ground were marked. Stone slabs have been found near some graves. Others were marked with wooden posts or boards connected to the head or foot of coffins. Loved ones likely held ceremonies to honor those laid to rest and continued to visit the burial ground following the ceremonies. Many believed the reburial was an important part of respecting and remembering those the remains belonged to.

A Place to Remember

In 2007, a memorial designed by **architect** Rodney Leon was completed. It's a tribute to the past, present, and future generations of Africans and African Americans. Writing on a memorial wall explains that the memorial is:

> "For all those who were lost
> For all those who were stolen
> For all those who were left behind
> For all those who are not forgotten."

There is also a visitor center for the African Burial Ground. Located on the ground floor of the Ted Weiss Federal Building, the tower built on the grounds, visitors can read about Africans' role in early New York as well as the story of the burial ground, past and present. Models of the unearthed findings, a movie, and various exhibits can also be viewed at the visitor center.

If you go to New York City, you can see the outdoor memorial at the **intersection** of African Burial Ground Way, which was formerly Elk Street, and Duane Street.

~ At the Monument ~

The African Burial Ground National Monument includes a gathering space for ceremonies and a chamber for quiet reflection. The Wall of Remembrance describes events involving the African Burial Ground's creation. Leon included many African symbols in the memorial as well. Visitors can follow a curving path that leads through a map of Africa, Europe, and North and South America. The center of the spiral is West Africa, where the ancestors of many African New Yorkers were from.

Today, people visit the monument to honor those buried there and to remember the role enslaved people played in building New York City.

The African Burial Ground helps us understand the past, but it can also help us learn about the present. Upon the discovery of the bones, it became important to the African American community of New York City to take ownership of the unearthing and research of those in the cemetery. These were their ancestors. Studying the remains and creating the memorials have helped people understand parts of history that otherwise may have been lost.

The 1991 discovery reminded many that the city of New York only became the great city that it is today because of the labors of African residents, whether enslaved, "half-free," or liberated. When the African Burial Ground National Monument was **dedicated** in 2007, it was the first to be dedicated to Africans of early New York.

|| Timeline of the African Burial Ground || |||

1673	1794	1795	1991	1993
Sara Van Borsum allows land she owned outside of New York City to be a burial ground for Africans.	The African Burial Ground is closed.	The African Burial Ground is divided up and sold.	Construction of a federal office building unearths the African Burial Ground's location.	The African Burial Ground is declared a National Historic Landmark.

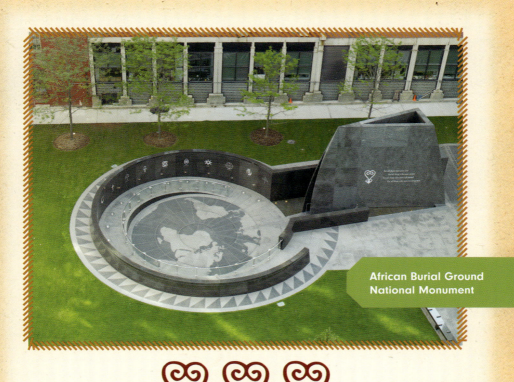

African Burial Ground National Monument

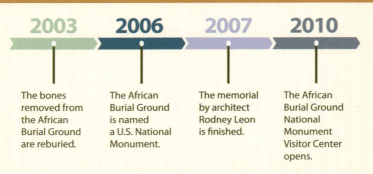

2003 The bones removed from the African Burial Ground are reburied.

2006 The African Burial Ground is named a U.S. National Monument.

2007 The memorial by architect Rodney Leon is finished.

2010 The African Burial Ground National Monument Visitor Center opens.

GLOSSARY

architect: a person who designs and guides a plan, project, or building

coffin: a box in which a dead person is buried

curfew: an order or law that requires people to be indoors after a certain time at night

dedicate: to officially open a place for honoring or remembering something

excavation: the act or process of digging and removing earth in order to find something

geneticist: a scientist who studies genetics, or things related to genes

indentured servant: one who signs a contract agreeing to work for a set period of time in exchange for passage to America

intersection: the spot where two or more streets meet or cross each other

malnutrition: the unhealthy condition that results from not eating enough food or not eating enough healthy food

musket: a type of long gun that was used by soldiers before the invention of the rifle

obliterate: to destroy something completely so that nothing is left

petition: to ask for something in a formal way, typically when a group of people come together to ask for something in writing

rebellion: an effort by many people to cause change, often by the use of protest or violence

FOR MORE INFORMATION

Books

Albee, Sarah. *Accidental Archaeologists.* New York, NY: Scholastic Press, 2020.

Uhl, Xina M. *A Primary Source Investigation of Slavery.* New York, NY: Rosen Central, 2019.

Websites

The African Burial Ground
www.gsa.gov/portal/content/101077
Read about the discovery that started it all.

African Burial Ground National Monument
www.nps.gov/afbg/index.htm
Find out more about the burial ground including how to visit it.

Publisher's note to educators and parents: Our editors have carefully reviewed these websites to ensure that they are suitable for students. Many websites change frequently, however, and we cannot guarantee that a site's future contents will continue to meet our high standards of quality and educational value. Be advised that students should be closely supervised whenever they access the internet.

31

INDEX

African Society 20

Bryant Park 23

Cobb Laboratory 6

Dutch East India Company 15

Dutch West India Company 12, 14, 15

environmental impact study 5

Howard University 6, 11, 22

James II 14

Leon, Rodney 26, 27, 29

monument 9, 21, 27, 28, 29

National Historic Landmark 22, 28

New Amsterdam 12, 13, 14

New Netherland 12, 13, 14, 15

Portuguese, Anthony 13

Rodrigues, Jan (Juan) 21

Ted Weiss Federal Building 26

Union Square 23

Van Borsum, Sara 18, 19, 28

Washington Square Park 23